Praise for Elizabeth Engstrom

On **Baggage Check**:
"The author is so deft at creating interesting, 3D characters that I was instantly hooked into Sweetann's plight (yes, Sweetann). Even the bad guys have depth and lives beyond the story. This is not a typical thriller which makes it much more interesting than the average shoot 'em up, and Sweetann is not a typical heroine. A guaranteed fun time."
    – Christina Lay, author of *Death is a Star*, editor at Shadow Spinners Books

On **Black Leather**:
A darkly seductive page-turner by a writer who knows how to put the erotic thrill into a thriller.
    —*DarkEcho*

An artfully written and highly recommended erotic and psychological suspense from first page to last.
    —*Midwest Book Review*

On **Suspicions**:
This is where she's at her best.
    —*Locus*

A spooky collection of tales.
    —*Publishers Weekly*

"Like many fine writers, Engstrom's stories are across all genres. Some can be termed sf, others as mystery or fantasy or horror, still others are simply "fiction." A few are light and humorous. Most are quietly dark, slightly skewed, angled toward that indescribable place just at the edge of shadow. All are worth reading. Many are worth pondering. By the end, at least one suspicion will definitely be confirmed: Elizabeth Engstrom is one of the best. No doubts."
    —*Cemetery Dance*

On **York's Moon**:

"*York's Moon* is so absorbing and unusual that you'll almost miss how beautifully written it is—almost. Elizabeth Engstrom's mesmerizing and unique style will draw you into a world of mystery, violence and heroic struggle. Ultimately, this story celebrates the uplifting power of the human spirit. Do not miss it."

—Susan Wiggs, bestselling author of *Marrying Daisy Bellamy*

"With quirky, engaging characters, *York's Moon* is as much about understanding the human condition as solving a murder mystery. I cannot imagine anyone but Liz Engstrom writing this fine novel."

—Terry Brooks, author of the *Shannara* series

On **The Northwoods Chronicles**:

A genre-blending exploration of love, aging, grief and sacrifice. Fast-paced, melancholy and beautiful, the overarching narrative binds a collection of good stories into a superb if unconventional novel.

—*Publishers Weekly*

"To read Elizabeth Engstrom is to be guided by the sure hand of an accomplished writer whose stories have the power to transfer readers to places both real and surreal. We believe in the unbelievable, marvel at worlds created between dream and reality, and reach for all that transcends the limits of our imagination."

—Gail Tsukiyama, author of *The Street of a Thousand Blossoms*

"From the ominous opening to the soaring conclusion, these braided stories – subtle and spooky and smart – will keep the reader spellbound.. The Northwoods is a scary place to live, but in Ms. Engstom's hands, it's a fabulous visit."

—Karen Joy Fowler, author of *The Jane Austen Book Club*

On *Lizzie Borden*:

Every door in the Borden house is metaphorically locked, and each room holds the terrible secrets of the occupant... Engstrom [moves] the reader inexorably toward the anticipated savage denouement.

—*Publishers Weekly*

Engstrom has woven a fascinating tale of a lonely, tormented and frustrated young woman.

—*Rocky Mountain News*

A real page-turner and white-knuckler. The tension mounts without letup.

—*Maui News*

Engstrom crafts a character with motivation, mental confusion and smoldering resentment, a woman who could stand unblinking in a shower of blood as she bludgeoned her parents to death.

—*Ogden Standard Examiner*

On *Lizard Wine*:

"*Lizard Wine* is the book your mother warned you about, sleek, nasty, perfectly focused, smart as hell, absolutely convincing, and utterly single-minded."

—Peter Straub, author of *Ghost Story*

"Excruciating suspense!"

—Bryce Courtenay, author of *The Power of One*

Supertaut storytelling.

—*Kirkus Reviews*

On *When Darkness Loves Us*:

A masterpiece, and one of the finest tragedies I've read in years.

—*Horror Show*

"Behind that soft-voiced style is power, is surprise, is... ferocity."

—Theodore Sturgeon

Books by Elizabeth Engstrom

Novels
When Darkness Loves Us
Black Ambrosia
Lizzie Borden
Lizard Wine
Black Leather
Candyland
The Northwoods Chronicles
York's Moon
Baggage Check

Collections of Short Fiction
Nightmare Flower
The Alchemy of Love
Suspicions

Nonfiction Books
Something Happened to Grandma
How to Write a Sizzling Sex Scene

Anthologies Edited
Word by Word (co-editor)
Imagination Fully Dilated (co-editor)
Imagination Fully Dilated vol. II (editor)
Dead on Demand (editor)
Pronto! Writings from Rome (co-editor)
Ship's Log: Writings at Sea (co-editor)
Lies and Limericks (co-editor)
Mota 9: Addiction (editor)

How to Write
a Sizzling Sex Scene

by Elizabeth Engstrom

IFD Publishing
P.O. Box 40776, Eugene, Oregon 97404 U.S.A.
www.ifdpublishing.com

Copyright © 2015 Elizabeth Engstrom
Cover and book design by Alan M. Clark
ISBN: 978-0-9965536-3-6

Originally Printed in the United States of America

How to Write
a Sizzling Sex Scene

by Elizabeth Engstrom

IFD

Publishing

Eugene, Oregon

Dedicated to Al Cratty

My inspiration for many things erotic

Acknowledgements

Thanks to all the writing conferences and conventions where the presentation of this information was honed, to all the students who attended my erotic writing weekends, to all my lovers who taught me the finer points of pleasure, and all the writing teachers and students over the years. May you all read this information, do plenty of research on your own in private, and then write your best erotic work.

Table of Contents

"Pornography is about dominance. Erotica is about mutuality." –Gloria Steinem

Foreword

I decided to write this small book right after I got yet another call from a writer's conference director asking me if I would come give my sex talk at her conference.

My sex talk.

For years, I've been teaching weekend workshops on writing erotica for women (and one memorable one for men—more on that later) and giving short conference-sized workshops on how to write well-crafted sex scenes. Sex scenes are crucial to good fiction; they're excellent opportunities to reveal character, and there's a simple structure to it. These classes are wildly popular, and they have made me an "in demand" instructor at writer's conferences and conventions all over the world.

In fact, occasionally I will walk down the hall at a writer's conference and hear furtive whispers: "There goes the sex writer."

Sex writer! As if I were a pornographer. I could be insulted, but I'm not; I'm amused.

The classroom is packed with expectant faces. What is she going to do? (What do they think? Unbutton my blouse?) What is she going to say? (What do they think? Run down a list of dirty words?)

I talk about writing. I talk about the sexual nature of their fictional characters. I talk about the three-act structure of a scene, and the three-act structure of a sex scene. I talk about practicing writing. I talk about vocabulary and what to call body parts. I talk about the difference between pornography and erotica. I talk about revealing character to the reader, and revealing character at a most vulnerable moment.

Those in the audience, they hear me—they're taking notes—but I know they're not thinking of their fictional characters. They're thinking of themselves. This is what makes these classes so popular. I don't use any dirty words. I don't name any body parts. I talk about writing, but they're all thinking of themselves. They think of themselves as fictional characters and they look at their sexuality. My class gives them permission to do that. And it's fun, because they can ask thinly veiled questions: "My character has this problem…" And we pretend she's talking about her character. I make light of it, and I can do that without insulting her, because we're not talking about her, we're talking about a character in her novel. She can laugh and learn and everybody else laughs and learns.

Sex is, after all, pretty funny.

Occasionally, it gets a little heavy, a little dicey, and I am always the first to hold up my hand and claim that I am not a therapist; I am a writer. This class (or seminar) is not about pain or healing your sexual issues. We're talking about fiction here. And even that gets a laugh.

Then I give them an assignment and ten minutes to practice what they've learned in the past hour. After ten minutes, I open the microphone and they line up to read the portion of a sex scene they've written.

It's hilarious. It's moving. It's astonishing. They have no problem saying those words, naming those body parts.

And we all go home thinking of ourselves and our sexual nature in a little different way. Certainly none of us ever looks at our fictional characters in the same way again; most of us look at our spousal units in a very good way later that evening.

I think that's the real reason these classes are so popular. Even though I don't talk dirty, I don't tell smutty jokes, I don't demonstrate anything vulgar on stage, everybody in the audience employs their largest sexual organ— their brain—for the hour and a half (or weekend) we're together, and they learn a little bit about human nature. Their nature. Which is what writing is all about: *Fearless, relentless introspection.*

Of course the writer in me is always worried that I'll drop dead some day soon and be remembered for giving the sex talk instead of the short stories, essays and novels that I so agonize over.

But in the meantime, I'll go to another writer's conference and give my "sex talk" and laugh and have fun, learn a little, teach a little, and best of all, spend time with other writers.

And now there's a book.

"Love making is much more than physical expression, it is a soulful dance of sensual wonder and euphoric amazement." —*T.F. Hodge*

First, a Comment

Chances are, I won't write another book about writing. This will be it—a specialized book for serious fiction writers who want to add depth to their characters. There are way too many books on writing out there, written by writers far more competent than I to disassemble fiction and label the parts. I know you're eager to get to the juicy sex stuff, but please indulge me for a moment while I say a few things about writing in what will probably be my only widespread opportunity to say them.

First, I believe that writing has chosen you instead of the other way around. I can't imagine that anyone in his/her right mind would choose this vocation. If you can put your pen down and walk away, I think you should. The rest of you are here because you have something important to say. You have a message. You may not be able to articulate it at the moment, but it burns within you, and the only thing you have found that quells the fire is writing.

But writing, it seems, is a profound responsibility. What should you write that lives up to the message you have to impart? It would be unseemly to write a thriller, or a bathtub romance, or a spy novel, or a murder mystery where people run around killing each other in terribly inventive ways when your message is so…so…*significant,* so *spiritual.* And a sex scene?!?! Good grief. How could you possibly write steamy sex scenes that members of your club, or church, or family will read?

Relax. The message you have doesn't need to be spelled out in black and white, you don't need to make it the central theme of your novel, and you certainly don't need to pound your reader on the head with it.

Here's the truth: *It doesn't matter what you write. Whatever you believe will show through.*

Your message is imparted to your readers through the emotions of your characters. Just like it does in your life. You can't hide who you are. Not for long, anyway.

You're the one choosing the nouns and verbs. You're the one who is putting your characters into some form of peril, you're the one who will help rescue them and see to their reward and/or comeuppance. Don't worry. You can write anything. You can write about living on Mars, or in the year 2168, or in the year 560 BC, and your message will still show through. You can write from the point of view of someone of the opposite sex, or a different species, or a mythical character. It doesn't matter, as long as your characters evince the *emotions* that your readers can identify with.

Emotion is your message.

Write what moves you. Write your passion. Write your heart. Don't write what you think you should write, what your friends, spousal unit, parents, agent, editor, or the recycling guy thinks you ought to write. Sometimes we don't have much of a choice about what we write, so write what is in you.

You and I as writers have a significant role in the evolution of society. We are the keepers of the literature, the chroniclers of our times. If we must be true to anything, we must be true to ourselves in our fiction. Let others write their stories the way they are to write them. Don't compare yourself. Just write yours.

All of this is easy for me to say and hard for you to do. Telling the truth is not easy. Good fiction has very good good guys and very bad bad guys. Writing bad guy stuff (not unlike writing a sex scene) is difficult, simply because you're admitting to God, your mother, and the rest of the world, that you know those words, know those procedures, have had those thoughts, those feelings. Those bad guys, while they're not you, they are *of* you. Writing is hard. Very hard. And that's our job. Don't whine, don't cheat, don't give in. Tackle it as the difficult task that it is and get it done.

Okay. Now to the good stuff.

Sex.

"Insights into erotic life belong to art, not education."
—Karl Kraus

Chapter 1 – Why Sex Scenes?

We're all sexual beings. Sex is one of the primary driving forces in our animal natures, in order to assure procreation and continuation of the species. We are mammals, after all. Nature has given each life form on this planet an amazing reproductive cycle; none more amazing than the human. Ever got a burr on your sock from walking through a field? That plant (aka weed) is counting on a furry animal (or sock) to walk by, grab one of its fertile seeds by mistake, and carry it far away to be planted in another place, to assure progeny. That's pretty amazing. It is to me, anyway. Wolves mate for life, because that's what it takes for them to assure their species. Rabbits breed like...well, like rabbits, because they're low on the food chain, and their survival assurance lies in their numbers.

Okay. As wonderful as nature is, a human's sexuality is just as wonderful, but mighty complicated.

There are as many sexual tastes as there are people. Some like it this way, some that way, some like it almost this way but with a little bit of that way. Sometimes we have sex when we're angry, sometimes when we're happy, sometimes when we're out in the woods, sometimes when we're in public, sometimes behind closed doors with all the lights off. Sometimes not. Different things turn people on. This is not news to you, after all, you're a sexual being, too, and that didn't begin when you said your marriage vows. It began the moment you took your birthing cry. Or before. We are mammals. It is in a mammal's nature to breed.

So if it's in our nature to have sex, and forces work counter to accomplishing that (what would my mother say, what would my husband say, nice girls don't have sex on the first date, it's raining, he smells funny, what if I get pregnant, he's my boyfriend's best friend, etc.), then we have conflict.

In fiction, *plot is conflict.*

Let's digress for a moment and talk about plot.

* * *

There is a natural structure to fiction that starts with a flawed individual who just cruises along in his usual world. He's happy. He is resistant to change (as we all are). He is the hero of his own story (again, as we all are), thinking that his thoughts, feelings, and opinions are the right ones to have.

Then trouble comes knocking on his door. He resists it. He doesn't want any trouble. But trouble is persistent. It knows the back door, it can slide through the crack in the window, and it knows his history, because chances are, that's where this trouble was born. Our protagonist ignores it, and then tries to ignore it, and then sweats over it until the final straw, when he thinks it will be easier to fix the problem than to continue to resist it. He thinks to himself (or out loud): "I'm going to go ahead and fix that thing once and for all."

But thanks to his flawed nature, it is a lot easier to accomplish in his head than it is in reality. He will wrestle with the external trouble at the same time he battles with his internal troubles until the point that he thinks he's never going to fix the problem, and in fact he might not even survive the attempt.

Even though he's flawed, he has gained a few skills over his lifetime, and once he gets out of the fear stage and begins to get control over himself, the tables turn in his favor. He begins to vanquish the foe, and in the end, as a result of the external conflict, he is forced to take a look at himself, at his flaws, and he is changed by what he sees. The very definition of fiction is that it must include *a protagonist who changes* over the course of the story.

This is a tiny little simplification of the protagonist's journey, and if you want more detail, there are many books you can read about the structure of fiction. To my mind, *The Writer's Journey* by Christopher Vogler is required reading, and that book will help you understand all that goes on in a work of fiction.

But back to the sex scene.

There are myriad opportunities for conflict in a character's life, not the least of which is the sexual encounter.

A sexual encounter is a deliciously rich character-revealing opportunity. Your character could be a captain of industry, proficient in every aspect of his life, but a bumbling tongue-tied fool when in the presence of a woman. Or the reverse. Perhaps he can't even hold down a job, is in debt up to his eyebrows, but even so, the ladies can't keep their hands off him. Or he's a sexual athlete. Or a disappointing disaster in the bedroom. Or anything in between.

Perhaps your female is a cougar to end all cougars, which masks her horrifying insecurity issues. Perhaps she over indulges in carnal pursuits as a result of some childhood trauma.

Character is revealed to the reader through thoughts, opinions, emotions and actions. The way your character treats a pet, a plant, a coworker, a child, or a family member is not necessarily the same way he/she is going to treat a lover. Placing your characters in the sexual arena, where they are at their most vulnerable, sometimes their most fragile, can be very revealing.

So the first reason you should include sex scenes is that they're custom-made for a work of fiction about complex mammals. Sex scenes are perfect character-revealing opportunities, and fiction, is, after all, about character.

The second reason is that everybody likes to read them. Don't you?

And the third reason is that these days, everybody expects them. Even if the story is about one guy living alone in a cabin in the arctic, the topic of sex is going to come up. If not in his thoughts, then in his dreams, memories, a flashback…in his history. Why else would a man be living alone in a cabin in the arctic, if not failed by love?

* * *

So now that we've established the need for a sex scene, or many sex scenes, in today's novel, why are they so hard to write? Why are so many of the sex scenes I read in novels so poorly written?

Here's my theory, based on years of teaching: writers don't practice writing them.

Writers practice writing dialogue. Writers practice writing conflict scenes, they choreograph fight scenes, they outline and rehash and plant clues and red herrings, but they don't like to practice writing the sex scenes.

Why not? Pick one of many reasons: A. They're afraid of offending and/or intriguing their mother, their aunt, their child, their boss, their next door neighbor, their spouse, or any one of a zillion other people. B. They're afraid of offending themselves (writing pornography). C. They're afraid of becoming aroused.

Well, first, you can't write the truth about the characters you're writing and maintain a fear of offending somebody. Your mother has had sex. Deal with it.

Second, you're not going to offend yourself once you know your personal boundaries. You write until you find them, and then you don't exceed them. It's that simple. More on that in the next chapter.

Third, becoming aroused is okay. In fact, it's a good

thing.

Listen. The purpose of writing well is to put your readers into the shoes of the character. You want your reader to cry when your character is sad, to laugh when things are funny. And your reader should become aroused when the character they're living with, identifying with, cheering for and empathizing with, is having some wonderful sex. It's okay for you to get aroused when you write it, too. Nobody is going to know, unless you tell them. So go ahead. Get into it. Enjoy yourself. Lord knows, there are few enough pleasures in the crafting of a novel.

The Work Harder Exercises

At the end of every chapter is an exercise designed to open your skills and your mind to the possibilities of sensual imagery, relationships, and all kinds of sexual encounters in fiction. I call these "Work Harder" Exercises because I want you to work hard on them, and whenever you feel a cliché coming on, I want you to delete it and work harder. Exercises aren't worth much if you don't put your best into them.

Work Harder Exercise #1:

Write a scene where your character is with his/her lover, outside in the sun on the first warm spring day. Overdose on sensory imagery. Use all five senses. Include dialogue. This doesn't have to include sex, this is all about sensory imagery.

"Though both erotica and pornography refer to verbal or pictorial representations of sexual behavior, they are as different as a room with doors open and one with doors locked. The first might be a home, but the second could only be a prison." —Gloria Steinem

Chapter 2 — Is it Erotica or Pornography?

We'd all like to be writing well-crafted sex scenes. Not very many of us want to be writing pornography. But what's the difference? Where's the line that distinguishes one from the other? It doesn't help that Webster defines erotica as pornography, and defines pornography as obscene art.

The problem is that the line is in a different place for everybody. One woman's erotica is another woman's pornography. So you, as the writer, as the artist, has to decide where the line is for you. If you write to please your agent, or your mailman, or your spouse, you'll not please your editor, or your plumber, or your mother. So please yourself instead.

Let's see if we can toy with a few definitions to help ease your mind.

What is erotica?

Eros, in Greek mythology, is the god of love.

When there's love, there's caring and interest in pleasing the partner. There is attention to detail. There is atmosphere and sensuality. Things slow down. People take their time.

There's no love in pornography. In pornography, body parts slap together until physical release. There's no tenderness. There's no real motivation for two people to have sex, except the sex act itself. There's pathos in that, which is something that can be used to our advantage as well.

Personally, I don't think erotica necessarily needs to deal with the sex act. Preparing an exquisite meal can be erotic in its sensuality, in its desire to please. A massage can be very erotic, though not at all sexual.

Think about getting a professional massage. It's slow, it's sensual. A practiced masseuse will never take her hand completely away from your body; she'll always be touching you somewhere, because you're naked and vulnerable. To take her hand completely away would leave you in a state of anxiety, however small, as to where she'll touch you next and when. There's no need for any anxiety at all while you're having a massage. That's professional attention to detail. Her hand motions are slow, her hands are well oiled for a smooth, deep rub. To me, that's erotic. A good masseuse loves what she does and gives a wonderful gift.

A bad massage—now *that's* obscene art.

* * *

So here's how you find the difference between erotica and pornography for you: Practice. Practice writing all kinds of sex scenes, from the woman's point of view, from the man's point of view, from the point of view of someone peeking in the window. Write happy sex, sad sex, pitiful sex, unsuccessful sex, religious sex, routine sex, instant sex, and write it until you feel comfortable with it.

Then push the envelope. Write until you reach your boundary with pornography. Go to the line. When you cross it, you'll know. You will recoil as if you've touched an electric fence, and the delete key won't work fast enough or erase completely enough.

Write until you touch upon that which you find distasteful, and then stop. Don't write past that. Discovering your boundaries is always liberating. It's like going to a buffet and knowing that you're not going to eat anything with chocolate in it. Chocolate is not an option (it gives you hives, let's say). The buffet is no less appetizing or appealing; there is just a section of it that is of no interest to you. A very small section, I might add.

So discover your boundaries, and then stay on the playing field. Everything on this side of that line is yours to think about, dream about, write about, laugh about, or even do, and you will know in your heart that you're not writing pornography. Someone, somewhere will object, but that's their problem, not yours. They're not interested in reading the book you're writing anyway.

At least you are not offending yourself.

Work Harder Exercise #2:

Write a Romeo & Juliet-type scene where two people spark electricity when they meet for the first time, but love is impossible between them. Write it from one person's point of view, then write the same scene from the other person's point of view. Remember, men look at women much differently than women look at men. Emphasize the tension between them because of their situation.

"Women are on the whole more sensual than sexual, men are more sexual than sensual." —Mai Zetterling

Chapter 3 — Size Doesn't Matter, but Point of View Does

I've been teaching weekend erotic writing seminars for women for a long time. I've been giving talks and workshops at writing conferences and conventions on writing a sex scene since for almost as long. I've talked with lots and lots of writers about their sex scenes, and there is one absolute that I have learned in the process: men and women look at sex differently.

This is key*: If you are a woman, and you think you know how a man thinks, you are wrong. If you are a man, and you think you know how a woman thinks, you are wrong.* This is not to say that a woman can't write from a man's point of view and vice versa, but it requires research, a good pal to vet your work, and a light touch. Men and women are different orders of the same species, and their thought processes, drives, motivations and methods are different from one another.

Obvious in life, right? Right. But what this means in writing the sex scene is that if you're writing from the female point of view, the sex must be very female, and the same for the male POV. So what are female attributes of a sex scene?

Speaking in generalities, women fantasize about having

intimate, significant, romantic sex in outlandish places.

Let's talk for a moment about biology.

Women are, biologically speaking, equipped to breed with a male, carry a child to term, then raise a helpless, hairless creature to maturity. They need help. As much as the independent female tries to talk herself into being as sexually liberated as any male, she isn't. It goes against her biology. Every time a woman opens herself up to having sex with a man (don't forget I'm speaking in generalities here), her body's instincts kick in to prepare for the coming child. She's going to be incapacitated for a while (no hunting/gathering). She needs a male to protect the cave entrance, to throw the slab of meat on the hearth, where she will fix it and make him a fine home while the baby nurses, toddles, and finally finds a little independence of its own.

Women for years have tried to have sex with their male friends, but it never works. Books have been written about it, movies have entertained it, to men it is the mystery of the ages. Sex always changes a relationship. Always. Biology kicks in after sex has been introduced, and the woman's nature is to cling to her mate. That's why she's hurt when he doesn't call afterwards. Even if she told him not to, she's still hurt.

So what do women look for in a man? Staying power, and I don't mean just in bed. They look for values. They look for substance. They look for a good provider, a man with moral fiber and one who will stand by the family.

They look for good genes, they look for the captain of the football team.

If you want to do a little research into the mating practices of the human beast, go to the mall, where the mating dance is at its most primitive. Teenagers, at the height of their sexual appetites, are prowling. The girls are made up perfectly, their clothes are trendy and tight, their hair is exactly right. They know that to attract a man, they must first attract his eye.

The boys are slouching around with their hats on backwards and the crotches of their pants down to their knees.

Ask a girl what she likes about her boyfriend? She'll say, "He's nice."

Ask a boy what he likes about his girlfriend? He'll say, "She's hot."

What are we to learn from this?

Point of view matters.

So what about the men? Men are built in the exact opposite way. If women want to have significant, meaningful sex in outlandish locations, men want to have an outrageous, good-times romp in the comfort of their own beds.

Men are built to broadcast seed. It's survival of the fittest. The head cheerleader always wants to breed with the captain of the football team, because he appears to have the best genes. Those men who view themselves with the best genes want to scatter them far and wide.

This is one of the reasons that a woman will live with a philandering husband, but not necessarily so the reverse.

How do women react to pornography? How do men? Why the difference?

Do your research. Scour the magazine racks for new research on this. Read one or two of the Venus/Mars books by John Gray and books by other authors who have similar takes on the situation. Watch television sitcoms. The best ones capitalize on this odd phenomenon of the gender gap. It's crucial to your writing.

One last tidbit of information I've learned in my years of writing fiction (and therefore being an amateur psychologist): Men and women view *everything* differently. Even the way they fall in love is different.

Here's the rule of thumb about love: *Women become attracted to the men they've fallen in love with; men fall in love with the women they're attracted to.*

Translation: go back to the mall.

The girls know they first have to become attractive to the boys for the boys to want to get to know them, to find out what sterling little girls they are, so the boys can fall in love with them.

The girls have a tendency to fall in love with the boys they hang out with. They get to know the boys first, and one day they realize that the nerdy guy who's been their best friend's best friend (or their boyfriend's best friend, or their brother's best friend) is suddenly very attractive. These two scenarios aren't confined to the mall. They go on in offices buildings and in neighborhoods all over the world every day.

Don't forget that we're mammals, and it is in a mammal's nature to breed. Put two mammals of the opposite sex in a room together long enough, and they're going to do it. Be advised. It takes moral fiber to resist, something our fictional characters don't necessarily have.

* * *

When you're writing a sex scene, both parties bring to the union their entire histories. They bring expectations, hurts, old decisions, prejudices, fetishes born of who-knows-what, shyness, aggressiveness, and an incredible array of agendas.

Make sure that if you're a man writing from the woman's point of view (or vice versa), that your female character's experience is female. Make sure you're using the correct vocabulary. Men and women think differently, act differently, talk differently, experience life differently. Use a little humility and do your research. Writing from the point of view of a member of the opposite sex is a lot harder than you think, and it's easy to spot a fake.

And speaking of point of view: choose it carefully. Play out this particular sex scene through the eyes and senses of one of the characters, not the narrator looking on from the end of the bed. And don't go back and forth between the characters, either. Slide inside the skin of one of your characters and tell us that person's complete, sensory experience. There's more on point of view in Chapter 11.

Work Harder Exercise #3:

Write a scene where a woman has a moment of profound affection for her husband of many years. Then write the same scene from his point of view.

"Never had he felt the joy of the word more sweetly, never had he known so clearly that Eros dwells in language." —Thomas Mann

Chapter 4 — The Simple Structure of a Sex Scene

Everything is written in a three-act structure. Anecdotes, jokes, stories, novels, plays, movies, sitcoms. Each one has a Setup, a Complication, and a Resolution.

Notice the next time you watch your favorite half-hour sitcom. Chances are, it will have three simultaneous storylines going, and each one will have a setup, a complication, and a resolution. Study this. (There's more on the three-act structure in Chapter 11.)

Likewise, scenes have a three-act structure, and sex scenes are no different.

Here's a joke. A bad joke to be sure, but one which will be easy to pick apart to label its parts:

A vulture tries to get on an airplane with a dead raccoon under each wing.

The flight attendant says, "I'm sorry sir, but only one carrion per passenger."

I know, I know. It's bad. But it's short.

The setup includes the protagonist, the antagonist and the conflict.

The complication augments the original conflict.

The resolution resolves the conflict. In the joke above, it's easy to see who is the protagonist, who is the antagonist, what is the potential conflict, and how it all resolves. A novel has the exact same structure, only longer. A sex scene has the exact same structure, too.

In a sex scene, the Setup is the Foreplay, the Complication is the Sex Act, and the Resolution we call Afterglow.

Let's take them one at a time.

Foreplay

This is what it's all about. Sexual tension. This is working with the sexual nature of your characters. You can't ignore it. It has been said that human beings have a sexual thought every seventy seconds. Think about that.

If your character is an adolescent with hormones rushing, and his English teacher is a well-formed, very pretty twenty-five year old, and he's sitting in class, with his attention focused on her for several hours every day, and he has a sexual thought every seventy seconds, within a few days, those sexual thoughts are naturally going to slide in her direction. He will focus on her, and it isn't going to be long before he's in love with her. He's spent way too much time fantasizing about her, in a very pleasurable way. He equates the visual image of her with the pleasurable feelings he gets in his thoughts.

Now put them in an empty classroom together after school, when she's trying to talk with him about his grades. He could be tongue tied and unresponsive in the face of her undivided attention, or he could possibly mistake the situation as an opportunity for advancement. Either way, sexual tension abounds. From his point of view, anyway, and maybe from hers as well.

Or Lady Chatterly watching the gardener out of her window day after day. Or the secretary watching her boss. Or the boss watching his secretary. The church secretary and the pastor. Two co-workers in adjoining cubicles. Same thing.

Proximity with anticipation = foreplay.

Act One: Setup: Foreplay.

Books, movies, season after season of dramatic television have been predicated upon foreplay. Longing. Yearning. Flirting. Resisting whatever trouble that succumbing to the sexual temptation will bring.

As human beings, whenever there are two people of opposite sex together (homosexuality brings its own sexual conflicts. At the moment, I'm restricting this to heterosexual issues), there is sexual tension. This is not to say sexual *attraction*, but sexual *tension*. There is always tension when there is possibility for miscommunication. Men and women speak the same language, they say the same words, but the interpretation is widely varied, both by what he says vs. what he means, and what he says vs. what she hears.

Sexual tension can easily grow into sexual attraction, and in fiction, it usually does. Whether that attraction culminates in any action is up to the author, but that question plays a great role in holding the interest of the reader.

Suspense is the art of drawing out the action, and keeps readers on the edge of their seats. Foreplay is all suspense. Will they? Won't they? Who (or what) will be the next thing to interfere with the consummation of their burning love?

Remember that readers are cheering for the characters. If they're made for each other and having a hard time coming to that conclusion, or resisting it, or myriad forces intervene, readers are frustrated, but full of hope. And when the opportunity finally arrives, it is a sweet moment to the reader.

Draw out the foreplay. Give your characters lots of sexual tension, lots of conflicts. Make the reader worry that they'll never be able to overcome all the obstacles in the way of their union.

Afterglow

We'll get to the sex act in a minute, but first I want to talk about Afterglow.

This is the time when all defenses are down. The act has been committed. The chase is over. The conquest has been won. All obstacles have been overcome. Both parties are completely vulnerable. There is no longer any reason to keep up the pretenses that got them into bed, is there?

Proximity + Satisfaction = Afterglow.

Act Three: Resolution: Afterglow

Afterglow is the resolution of the sex scene.

Afterglow is the secret ingredient to a satisfying sex scene. This is the choicest opportunity to reveal character that you will ever have, and most authors just skip over it. The couple hits the sheets and that's the end of the chapter.

Too bad.

What people do in that vulnerable moment of afterglow tells the reader much. Does he lie there wondering how long he has to cuddle her before he can go home without hurting her feelings (and thereby foiling his chances for another encounter)? Does he get up and bring her a warm moist towel? Does he whisper sweet nothings in her ear, make her laugh, tell her he loves her? Does he turn over and start to snore immediately? Does he get up, put his pants on and propose? (Some things men need to do with their pants on, I'm told.) Does he start talking about the wisdom of opening up their relationship to dating other people? Does he just get up without a word, grab his pants and leave? Does he pick a fight? And how does he feel? Good? Bad? Guilty? Angry? Determined never to let himself be led astray again? Is he proud of his performance or ashamed?

Does she get up and start cooking? Does she cry? Does she cling to him with desperation? Does she get right up, put on her jeans and leave? Does she pick a fight? Does she turn away from him and chew on a fingernail? Does she turn toward him and give him loving attention? Does she cover herself up in modesty? Does she immediately start making lists in her head of things to do at the office? How does she feel? Sexy? Stupid? Loving and loved? Like a loser? Guilty? Angry? Full of remorse? Afraid he won't respect her or ever call her again? Afraid she's pregnant or just contracted a disease?

Was the encounter satisfying, utilitarian or pathetic?

We're complex creatures, and we have sex for many reasons. Sometimes passion hits people right in the middle of a raging argument, and when the sex is over, they pick up fighting right where they left off. I know a of woman who is so afraid of getting pregnant, that she makes her husband wear two condoms in addition to using a spermicidal jelly whenever they have sex, and she also takes the pill. What do you suppose their afterglow is like? What do you suppose their foreplay is like? What do you suppose their sex is like?

If you ignore the Afterglow portion of a sex scene, you lose the most interesting part of a sex scene. You fail to capture an important moment in the lives of your characters. In a scene that has three parts: setup, complication, and resolution, you lose one third. The *best* third. Don't get them between the sheets and then cut to the next day or the next chapter. See it through.

The sex scene doesn't just happen spontaneously in a novel, just like it does not happen spontaneously in life. It has to be correctly motivated and appropriately placed. The characters spend a lot of time getting to it, shouldn't we know how they feel about it afterwards? I mean *immediately* afterwards. They can talk themselves into thinking they don't feel anything the following day or week, but there's no cheating on their emotional state immediately afterward.

Sex

Okay. Here we are, and it's taken us all these pages to lead up to it.

Act Two: Complication: Sex

It's not a coincidence that the sex act is a complication. Here's the truth about the sex part of the sex scene as I see it.

A. It's mostly choreography.

B. It's totally optional.

Remember earlier when we were talking about the differences between erotica and pornography? You can write an amazingly hot sex scene using sizzling foreplay and emotion-charged afterglow, and you need never enter the realm of the sex scene if you don't want to. This is how important the afterglow is; it is so important that you can completely give up the sex part and the reader will be satisfied. They don't need to see the dance. Unless something really unusual happens during the sex, readers pretty much know what's going on. What they want to know is how the characters feel about it after.

But if you want to write the sex part, please do. It's fun to write. It's fun to read. It's just not necessary.

Writing the sex scene is all technical stuff. There's

nothing worse than reading a good sex scene and getting really involved, and then one of the characters throws a leg somewhere illogical or anatomically impossible. The reader stops and scratches her head. Oops. Magic gone. Another opportunity lost.

So you must be absolutely correct with your choreography. The things they do, in the order and way they do them must work. Take your time. Include all manner of sensory details. Let your reader in on the intimate details of what your point of view character is feeling, smelling, tasting, feeling.

Work within your boundaries. The sex act part of your scene can be tasteful and erotic, emotional and moving. It can also be crude and disgusting if you're not careful. You have to practice. Practice erotic, emotional and moving. Try out crude and disgusting so you know what it looks like and feels like to write. Practice, practice, practice.

Work Harder Exercise #4:

Write an afterglow scene where a young man has just had sex for the first time and feels religious guilt about it. Then write it from the point of view of the woman who seduced him.

"Even on the level of simple physical sensation and mood, making love surely resembles having an epileptic fit at least as much as, if not more than, it does eating a meal or conversing with someone." —Susan Sontag

Chapter 5 — What Do You Call Body Parts?

Putting a word, a name, to genitalia is the crux of the sensitive issue about writing sex scenes. These are parts that are not normally discussed in mixed company, and in fact, are kept modestly hidden from view. If you were writing a cooking scene, you would have no problem putting the chopped peppers into the frying pan. But somehow, putting the erect penis into the vagina is a completely different thing, and it is that for two reasons. First, penis and vagina are not very romantic words (neither is "putting"), and second, there's lot more to it than that.

So if you wrap that simple act up with all the rest of the motivation, atmosphere, and personality that goes with it, and then add some sexy names for those parts, then everybody is uncomfortable, because there are many names for those parts, and none of them are acceptable for polite dinner table conversation.

I thought I'd include a list of synonyms for both penis and vagina in this chapter as a fun thing to do. To research it, I went to the internet and did a search for "synonyms vagina" and "synonyms penis" and was amazed, delighted, then horrified and outraged at what I found. So I decided not to use any of the thousands of synonyms I found, and let you discover them for yourself. If you want. I don't necessarily recommend it. Ick.

Instead, look to your characters for their vocabularies. Every word you use in a book should be one that your character knows. If you're writing an historical piece, be careful that you don't use modern language. If you're writing a young adult novel, you will use a vocabulary appropriate to the age range of the characters in the book as well as the readers. And when you're writing a sex scene, you'll use the vocabulary that your characters would use.

For example, if two crack addicts are having a go at each other in the alley behind a Chinese restaurant, they're going to have certain terminology that they will use, and chances are, it is different terminology than two gynecologists would use if they were making love. Which is different from what you and your partner say when you engage in that activity.

So as with all things, you must put yourself into the mindset of your point of view character and use his/her terminology. Sometimes that's street language, sometimes that's clinical language, sometimes that's inventive, fun, personality-driven talk. Perhaps they have nicknames for their own or each others' private parts. It's not unheard of, you know. This is another way of revealing character to your readers. If you are designing a character who must sail a boat from Honolulu to San Francisco, you will design that character with plenty of sailing experience—

most likely beginning when he or she was a child. That character will know all the sailing terminology, and use it with facility. It is a part of his/her vocabulary.

The characters in your book or story that are going to engage in a little erotic endeavor also have erotic pasts that impact upon their present. That past includes a vocabulary, and that vocabulary includes words for body parts. Reach into your characters' pasts and find out how they came to know those words and how they choose to use them. Remember that these characters are not you. They are completely different, and have different sexual tastes, preferences, and weirdnesses. Capitalize upon that.

Your family and friends will understand that those aren't your words, they're the words of your characters. Well, they will at least pretend to understand, if you insist.

* * *

Here's another option: write your sex scene without naming any body parts at all. It can be done—it can be done sensitively, gracefully, sensuously, erotically, and well—and all it takes is practice.

Speaking of which…

Work Harder Exercise #5:

Write a scene where a point of view female character is scheming to be at the right place and the right time to "accidentally" meet a guy she wants to start something with. He owns a series of massage therapy clinics, and she is a park maintenance worker. Then write the same scene from his POV.

"If you believe in the soul, do not clutch at sensual sweetness before it is ripe on the slow tree of cause and effect." —Ralph Waldo Emerson

Chapter 6 — Practicing

There's a secret to writing good sex scenes. It's the same secret to writing good dialogue. Or good characterization, or well-paced plots. I know you already know the secret, though you want me to give you a magic formula. There is no magic formula. The secret is: practice.

Most people think that because they can talk, and they have a computer, they can write. Well, I can read, and I have a piano, but that doesn't mean I can sing. And those who sing professionally practice a lot. A lot. Hours every day. Lots of scales, lots of songs, lots of notes streaming out of their mouths to fade into the ether. Lots of mistakes. Lots of doing over. Lots of drilling over and over and over until they get it right.

But writers want to hold on to their practice efforts. They think they can, or should be able to, sell everything they've ever put down on paper. Writers never throw their writings away on purpose. By accident, perhaps. In a rage, perhaps (always regretted). In a fit of despair, perhaps (always leading to deeper despair). But we never hit "select all" and then "delete" with clear head. Just the thought of it sends spasms through my psyche.

Tony Hillerman once said he has a whole file cabinet

drawer full of first chapters that never went anywhere. Why does he keep them? I don't know. I guess he thinks he might use one someday.

There is a story that has reached legendary proportions about Ray Bradbury and Robert Heinlein, two icons in the science fiction industry. Lore has it that the two sat down in front of the fireplace one evening with a bottle of brandy, and over the hours, each burned one million unpublished words.

There are many lessons in that extraordinary image.

I'm not advocating that you delete your work or clean out the filing cabinet and throw everything away. I am saying that many words will flow from your fingers before you get it right. And once having got it right, you have to continue to practice to keep getting it right. Because each project is different with its different problems.

Nobody ever writes a practice novel on purpose. It turns out that most of us have written practice novels, but while we're in the middle of them, we're certain the novel we're writing is so fresh, inventive and never before told, that it will sell and make us a billion bucks. We write straight out of the chute, with fresh degrees, or fresh retirement time, or fresh envy for the New York Times best selling authors, and believe that with no practice, with a first draft tucked under our arms, we can storm the publishing industry and land at the top of the heap.

Well, sometimes that happens. And sometimes people win the lottery. But most of us who are working writers, making a living at it, work hard every day, produce pages every day, and have done so for years and years. Who gets rich from it and who dies broke seems to be largely up to the whim of the fates, but one thing is certain: you will not write a good book without practicing your craft.

I have a tendency to gently tell my students, "It's generally not the first book written that sells first." Translation: Your first book was for practice, and, by the way, it was far too autobiographical. Learn from it and get on with writing the next one.

Time is always an issue for writers. If you never have enough time, then turn off the television, turn off the video game, and use that time to read, write, or think about writing. Driving time. Bathing time. Relaxing time. Take a notebook with you wherever you go, and while you're sitting in the dentist's waiting room, instead of reading National Geographic, practice writing a dialogue scene between the woman sitting next to you and a guy who is trying to seduce her. Or is trying to pressure her into not calling the cops after he just ran into her car. Or is trying to guilt her into lending him some money. Practice dialogue. Practice suspense. Practice revealing character while setting a scene. Practice writing.

And practice writing your sex scenes.

Write foreplay and afterglow scenes between your neighbors. Between your coworkers. Between the dentist and the guy in the post office. Practice with people in all socio-economic arenas, people with diverse interests, passions, fetishes, interests. Practice with people of different ethnic backgrounds, people with different levels of couth, different vocabularies. Practice hooking them up in a variety of settings, with a variety of problems inherent in those settings. Give them personal problems, dozens of reasons why they can't get together, and help them overcome those obstacles. Practice with old people, young people, May/December people. Practice with people who lived in the 1700s and in the year 2097. Practice with people who live in the jungle, in the desert, in Manhattan, on Mars. Practice, practice, and never, ever, stop practicing. Not until the Reaper stills your fingers.

And then only under protest.

Critique Groups

Not every professional writer is a fan of critique groups, but I am, under the appropriate circumstances. Actually, there is only one real criterion for whether or not you ought to be in a writer's group: if it works for you, you should. If it doesn't, quit. But before you quit forever because the first group was a little harsh with its criticism, try several groups, or combinations of writers. It could be that you just hadn't found a good match. Yet.

There are many formats to choose from. They range from three people to thirty people. They meet weekly, twice a month or monthly. Participants read their work aloud, or they hand out copies. Whatever works for you, here are my guidelines for having success in a writer's group.

Commit yourself to attending ten sessions, even if you get your ego bruised the first night. Unless the writers are unusually cruel, or you have nothing in common with them, stick it out and learn something.

Commit yourself to taking something to share (either read aloud or pass around, depending on the group format) *every single session.* This gives you a writing deadline. If you're not gasping your last, you need to be at that meeting.

Make sure you can commit to ten sessions. If your schedule is such that you can only produce enough for a bi-weekly session, then don't commit to a weekly session. Find a group (or organize one) that suits your needs. Don't try to hammer yourself into a group that doesn't fit.

Make sure there is some sort of time limit on the oral critiques. One minute or two minutes is fine; fifteen minutes is not. The groups that are the most successful use a timer for their critique sessions (and their readings as well). This minimizes the ego factor.

Take what constructive criticism you need and leave the rest. Remember that you are the author and therefore the author-ity on your work. Nobody else knows your vision, nobody else knows your long-range plan. Listen carefully to what they say, adopt the good suggestions and ignore the others. But for goodness' sake, don't argue, disclaim or defend your work. It needs to stand on its own. You can't explain it to those who buy your book. The necessary information needs to be on the page.

Be in charge of getting your own value out of the group. Don't think you're there to help all the other writers. Be selfish and squeeze every ounce of value you can from your group. While you're there to learn to write better, you're also there to learn to critique yourself objectively by learning to critique others. If everybody is equally selfish and dedicated to sucking the sweet juice from the group, it will work.

Don't let the group sidetrack into gossip, cookies, vacation photos, market reports, and industry-bashing. If that needs to take place (and sometimes it does), leave it for the meeting-after-the-meeting when you all go out for coffee and pie. If you need to be the one to police the group, do it.

Choose a group (or organize one) that meets your needs artistically. If you don't feel comfortable critiquing poetry, then don't join a group that includes poetry. But don't limit yourself to a group that writes Westerns, for example. Good fiction is good fiction, no matter the genre.

When critiquing, be kind. Try to bestow one orchid for every onion you have to deal out. You'll appreciate encouragement when the others have harsh things to say about your work. And they will. If it were perfect, it would be published. See Chapter 11 for a tried-and-true format for a critique group.

Conferences and Conventions

I am a great advocate for the new writer attending

conferences and conventions. There is a wealth of information to be had, along with networking, meeting people (writing is a solitary endeavor; make some friends with a similar passion for it. You'll find that you have more in common than you can imagine), and attending a good one will give you just the right amount of constructive envy to get you back on track.

I am also an advocate of joining a national writing organization, and attending their regional, national and international conferences and conventions. Listings of these organizations can be found in Writers Market, at your local library, or search the Internet. If you're writing romance novels, for example, you should join the Romance Writers of America. You'll get far more than your money's worth in publications, support, marketing information, and usually a local chapter to help you put it all into practice. Ditto science fiction, mystery, western, or just about any other genre you can imagine. Not writing in a genre? Then join a regional writer's organization and go to those conventions and/or conferences. Get out. Breathe some fresh air. Make some new friends. Study them closely. Ask them some embarrassingly personal, probing questions. Write down their answers. Go home and make up stories about them (giving them fictional names), sexy or otherwise. See how much fun this can be?

Work Harder Exercise #6:

Write a scene where a point of view male character is trying to avoid the woman he picked up in a bar the previous night. She's a psychologist and he's a professional dog-walker. And then, of course, write the scene from her POV.

"Art is the accomplice of love. Take love away and there is no longer art." —Rémy De Gourmont

Chapter 7 — Organizing an Erotic Writing Group

Writing sensual fiction will provide an interesting and important depth to your overall prose. Most writers fail to put enough sensory details into their work, and sensory details help the reader slide into the character's skin and experience the fullness of the story right along with them.

If you were to analyze the latest chapter of a book you wrote, or the last ten pages of a short story, you are likely to notice that you mention how things look many times, but never mention how something smells. We have five senses. Use them all. Your readers will accumulate all the sensory details that you include and that helps them slide into the shoes (or between the sheets) with your characters, helping to make the scene a success. Make it a point to include a sensory image in every paragraph of anything you write, most importantly a scene as sensory as one that includes romance. Use all five senses purposefully.

When you belong to an erotic writing group, you concentrate on those sensory details, and it will not only give you another writing deadline to meet, but it will give you feedback on your practice scenes. This is where you could break loose a little bit and experiment, because everybody else in the group is taking equal chances. If someone isn't contributing their writing—their blood sweat and tears—but only comes for the reading and/or critiquing, they must go. We had a rule in our writing group: If you miss three weeks in a row, unless you're on your deathbed or have a true emergency, you lose your seat. And there was no excuse at all for coming to the group without something to read. We were each exposing ourselves, being vulnerable in front of other writers; it was mandatory that we all do it to keep on equal footing.

In your erotic writing group, you might have three to seven members; hopefully it will be a mixed-gender group so you can get male/female responses to your writing. It doesn't have to center around writing sex scenes, either. As I said before, I think there's something very erotic about sailing, gardening, grooming a horse, preparing food to eat. Erotic to me has less to do with sex than the sensory imagery and attention to detail.

Meet monthly in a secure location without telephones, intrusions or eavesdroppers. Take it seriously. Write with passion. Be kind in your critiques. Remember: the only thing that will teach you to write is writing. Classes, books, seminars, conferences and conventions are all fine, but they won't teach you to write. To learn that, you must put your butt in the chair and write, rewrite, have your work edited, and then write some more. Practice.

In the 1980s, a group of middle-aged women in California started writing erotica for their own amusement. One day they realized they had a body of work that was so good, they just had to shared it with the world at large.

Celestial Arts Press published *Ladies Own Erotica* by The Kensington Ladies Erotica Society. The women all used pseudonyms and they went on tour wearing feathered masks. It was followed by another volume, *Look Homeward Erotica.* I adore those two books. I don't know what the Kensington Ladies are doing these days, but I hope they're sticking with it. To me, they blasted open the whole erotica genre and made it appropriate for all. Erotica went from usually tawdry to occasionally exquisite. We owe them.

In your erotic writing group, you can have class assignments. Here are some ideas to kick start your group.

Write the scene of a woman preparing for her first date with a man she had been lusting after for years.

Write the same scene from his point of view.

Write an afterglow scene of two newlyweds when he is to go off to war within hours.

Write the same scene from the other person's point of view.

Write a scene starting with this sentence: Only six people came to the wake, and two of them weren't old enough to drink. (Remember: pick your point of view carefully, pay attention to detail and sensory imagery along with conflict and characterization.)

Write the scene of a private, personal, long-anticipated picnic held in a hay loft.

Spend a group session designing a character together, then come up with a first line for your scene and each of you go home to write it. Make certain that the character (as all fictional characters), is just a little bit larger than life.

You get the idea. The point is to challenge yourselves into practicing outside your comfort zone, writing things that tax your imagination. Sometimes these little exercises turn into short stories. Sometimes they turn into novels. Sometimes they're just practice scenes which will be thrown away (or stuffed into the file cabinet until your heirs go through your papers). Sometimes they'll contain a kernel of something so good that you'll keep it in your Creative Compost File (See Chapter 11) and revisit it some day. Practice is never wasted. There's always something to be learned by putting pen to paper. Even if it's just learning about yourself. *Especially* if it's learning about yourself.

Work Harder Exercise #7:

Write an afterglow scene from the female point of view of a woman married to the same man for thirty-five years. They're both retired attorneys. Use all five senses. And then write from the opposite POV. Pay attention to those sensory details.

"The erotic does not end in spastic contractions and reflex discharges; it transcends them, to reach into the ethereal realms of memory and feeling, like a note that reverberates long after the string has pulsated." —*F. Gonzalez-Crussi*

Chapter 8 — Organizing an Erotic Writing Weekend

Okay, so your erotic writing group is in full swing, you've been meeting long enough to be able to trust one another, and you're ready for a new adventure in the world of erotic literature. Try going on an erotic writing weekend.

You don't have to be holed up in a hotel suite, although I have done that and it has worked very well indeed (room service and all). Some place beautiful always works best, especially at a time of year when writers can walk while contemplating and commune with their muses in an environment flush with sensory details.

You may have a weekend sleepover, or you may have everybody go home in the evening, but pay attention to the environment, the food, the writing spaces, and prepare carefully the writing exercises or other purpose of the time spent together. There must be nourishing food, plenty of snacks, and accommodating writing nooks and surfaces. (Potluck works better than going out to restaurants.) There must be places for the writers to wander while mulling things over. And there must be plenty of light. If affordable, go away. Make it a truly special event. Surely there are resorts within an hour or two that would be conducive.

Bring candles, snacks that might be of interesting texture or flavor, and wear fabrics that evoke erotic sensory imagery. Pay attention to the atmosphere of your writing space when you make arrangements.

If you have ground rules, state them clearly at the opening, so everybody understands.

Assign exercises, break to write, then reconvene the group to read what they've written, and gain some mild feedback. Remember, in a group like this, everyone is sharing first-draft work, so while writing on demand usually raises the bar on the quality of the work, a careless remark can so discourage a writer that the weekend (or more) could be lost for them. So don't refer to this as critiquing. Keep it to gentle feedback.

An erotic writing weekend is loads of fun, mostly because of the group dynamics. Sex is pretty funny, if you're writing sex scenes, and to produce a nice sized body of work in two or three days always makes writers high. You might even work in a field trip to an interesting location. Hmmm.... What might that look like? Use your imagination.

In the next chapter, I discuss what I've done in my erotic writing weekends. Use that as a starting place for your curriculum, but make your event your own.

Work Harder Exercise #8:

Write an afterglow scene from the male point of view of a man on his honeymoon. He's an ironworker and she works in a laundry. Then write it again. You get the drill by now, I think.

"Sex is an emotion in motion." —Mae West

Chapter 9 — My Weekend Workshops (Including the Memorable One for Men)

The erotic writing weekends I have been teaching started with a quest to discover what made good erotic writing. I was in the middle of a book and needed some help to make certain scenes very erotic, but like most writers, I was afraid of it. I didn't like what I saw in the bookstores or at the library, so being a teacher at heart, I held a class, and hoped that what I knew would be more than what the class knew, and then we could puzzle a few other things out together.

It worked. And I've been staging these weekends (for women only) for years. They're fabulous.

They're usually held in a palatial home or resort with plenty of beds. Sometimes, when a place like that isn't available, we go home at night, but the preference is to stay together all weekend. Sometimes writers like to write in the middle of the night. We get together on Friday evening, and adjourn sometime around noon on Sunday. Depending on the facility, attendance is limited to fewer than twelve women.

Here are the ground rules:

We never mention names when we're talking about our personal experiences. We use the generic term "My lover." Never "my husband," or "my boyfriend," or "my boyfriend three boyfriends ago," or "my girlfriend," or "Greg." We don't ever need to know specifically who anyone is talking about, because sometimes we know these people. Sometimes we know them very well, and too much information is... well, too much information. So we always use the anonymous "my lover."

There will be nothing written and then read during the weekend that has to do with animals, children or violence in a sexual way. They may write it at home if they wish, but I don't want to hear about it.

This is not about healing sexual trauma, except in an indirect way. We are here to write erotica, it is not a group therapy session.

No criticism, just gentle feedback. We're reading first-draft work.

The curriculum is simple. I give assignments, we write, then we read. The first assignment has to do with describing a sense. This is incredibly difficult to do. There's usually an array of munchies on the table, and participants gravitate toward taste. But to describe the taste of a cherry lifesaver when you can't use the words "cherry" or "sweet" is difficult. Ditto describing the feel of silk or the sound of the wind in the trees. This is the Friday night warm-up, and we write for a half hour or so, then talk about writing, and I always try to steer the conversation back into the sexual arena. If there is wine involved, it can get very, very funny.

The next exercise usually starts Saturday morning after breakfast. This is the foreplay scene, and we take an hour and a half to write it. After lunch we write the afterglow scene. Some people choose to use the same setting and same characters as with the foreplay scene; some choose something completely different. Later in the day we write the sex scene, and I encourage everybody to participate. Usually, by this time, participants have grown to know each other, feel safe, and are loosened up enough to be willing to tackle it. If not, that's fine. I'm not there to force somebody to write or to hear anything that they don't want to hear. We write, and then we read. Then everybody leaves or goes to bed exhausted but undeniably satisfied.

Those who used the same setting now have a complete sex scene, from foreplay, through the sex act, and into the afterglow.

The next morning we write "an erotic scene" that has nothing to do with sex.

This is the key scene, and the purpose of the whole weekend. Everybody is fresh on Sunday morning, our senses have been awakened by the previous writings, and the work that comes from this exercise is almost invariably exquisite.

People blossom at these weekends. Their writing takes enormous leaps forward. The participants learn things about themselves and each other and the sexual nature of humans that they would have no other opportunity to learn. Along with that, we eat well and laugh a lot. What could be better?

One time, some male friends enthusiastically encouraged me to hold an erotic writing weekend for men. Of course none of the men who so fervently encouraged me to do this registered for the class. I had a full class, and preparations were all ready for the weekend at a beautiful home, when the night before, I had as close as I have ever gotten to a panic attack. What if one of them is gay, and wants to write gay sex, and the others don't want to hear it? It was something I didn't feel prepared to deal with. I have lots of lesbians in my classes, and nobody seems to mind hearing about lesbian sex, and lesbians don't mind hearing about hetero sex, but I know that most straight men don't want to hear about gay male sex.

I needn't have worried. All the men who took that class were serious writers endeavoring to learn more about their craft. The fact remained, however, that I spent a weekend holed up with ten men, writing about sex. And not all of the things that I prepared as examples and as exercises worked well for them, because, of course, the things that men find erotic are completely different from the things that women find erotic.

We all learned a lot that weekend. Mostly, I learned not to do that again.

Work Harder Exercise #9:

Write a scene where a powerful CEO is seducing his single-mother secretary. Then write it from her point of view. Watch their vocabularies.

"In literary representation, the distinction between the genuinely erotic and the licentious is a distinction not of subject-matter, but of perspective. The genuinely erotic work is one which invites the reader to re-create in imagination the first-person point of view of someone party to an erotic encounter. The pornographic work retains as a rule the third-person perspective of the voyeuristic observer." —Roger Scruton

Chapter 10 — Hmmm. What if I like doing this a little too much?

Relax. I told you that this was fun.

Erotic writing is coming into its own these days. There are many anthologies that are buying erotic literature (short stories), and novels of all sorts are including more and more explicit sex scenes. Websites abound that publish erotic literature, and there are many publishers now who specialize in one or another type of sexually-charged stories and books. As your body of work accumulates, as you begin to enjoy this type of writing and get better at it, you can begin to investigate the markets and sell a few pieces now and then. Go to the bookstore and ask about erotic literature. Buy some. See what's being published and by whom. Then submit some stories. You can also collect your stories and approach a publisher with a complete volume.

You may also write for the sex market. I am not an

expert in this area, because I've not yet published anything other than under my own name, but many writers carry several pseudonyms. The market for X-rated literature will never wane, especially with the explosion of the Internet. Writing pornography is a business that presumably pays well. *How to Write Erotica* by Valerie Kelly—an unfortunate title in my opinion—is about writing for the sex market, and I'm sure there are other manuals out there on the subject. Do your research, just as you would with any other writing endeavor, and give it your best. There is a huge market for X-rated novels, letters, short stories and screenplays.

Be careful that you can do this and still respect yourself in the morning. If you're compromising your integrity with your writing or anything else in your life, chances are, while you may become a successful writer, you may discover that you have become a less than successful person.

There is another market for erotic literature, and that is the private one, between you and your mate. I believe that every professional dancer ought to know a little ballet, a little ballroom, a little soft-shoe. I also believe that every professional writer ought to be able to pull off a letter to the editor, a Valentine's Day poem, a short story, an essay, and eventually a book-length work of memoir, narrative non-fiction or fiction. And a nice erotic piece to be read by candlelight on one of those special evenings is a nice little treat for two. Don't be shy.

Make it very personal. Make it very intimate. You'll both love it.

Work Harder Exercise #10:

Write the intimate rendezvous you've always fantasized about. Foreplay, sex, aferglow.

"There is no art without Eros." —*Max Frisch*

Chapter 11 — More about Writing Fiction in General

Since this is likely the only book I will write about writing, I am including some snapshot information about writing fiction in general. There is nothing here that you won't find a zillion other places, but perhaps you will receive what I call a "golden nugget" or a realization because of the way I phrase something, or because you're reading this at the perfect time, while you are wrestling with a problem spot mid-project.

If you're new to writing, my advice is to read all you can about the process, go to as many local, regional, national and even international writing conferences you can for about two years, and network your little heart out. Attend classes, workshops, meet people, listen, learn, and practice. And then let it all sink in and write your best work and learn from being edited.

Meanwhile, here is a tiny bit of information that many, many other books on writing can expand upon.

Plot

Plot is conflict. I don't know of another decent definition of plot. When you write, you must have a conflict in every paragraph and tension in every sentence. *Fiction is about people in trouble. When the trouble is over, the story is over.* As a result of the trouble, the character has learned something about himself, or changed something about himself.

Writing fiction is a balancing act of character and plot. Too much character can corrupt the pace of the story; too much plot, and the reader loses anyone to care about.

Remember this: the reader must have a rooting interest in the central character (the protagonist). We must care about this person, even if it's to dislike or despise him. Without an emotional connection between the reader and the protagonist there is no story.

Whether you're plotting a short story or a novel, both need all the requisite elements of fiction: a protagonist, an antagonist, and a major point of conflict. The bigger, more complex the conflict, the stronger the characters. No matter how lovely and sympathetic your protagonist, *your story is only as strong as your antagonist.*

Your protagonist is always a reluctant hero. He is flawed, which is to say he is human. He is dragged out of his comfortable world into uncertainty. He changes internally because he is forced to look at his flaws as a result of the conflict presented by the antagonist. This conflict is the stimulation to his character growth. There should be internal conflict and external conflict *in every scene.*

Fiction is comprised of three acts: Act One: the Setup, Act Two: the Complication, and Act Three: the Resolution.

Act One shows the protagonist before the trouble

starts, in his comfortable world, but with myriad problems. Act One ends when the protagonist is so tired of avoiding the impending problem that he believes it is easier to fix the problem than to continue to avoid it. This is when he embarks upon his Quest. By the end of Act One, all the major players have been introduced, as well as the major point of conflict.

Act One places the conflict into the world of the protagonist. It is here the reader sees the impossibility of the situation, how high a mountain must be climbed. As we meet the players he is to interact with, we make judgments about these people—are they useful to the protagonist, or do they add to his many conflicts? The central conflict materializes before us (and the protagonist) and may increase in complexity because of who the protagonist is, and the people around him, and what's being asked of him. Act One is the building block upon which this story is going to stand. It's the first date. You want to get it right.

Act Two complicates every tiny point of conflict introduced in Act One. At the end of Act Two, the protagonist and reader alike are certain he will never be able to fix the problem. At the end of Act Two is the Darkest Moment.

In Act Two think: development. This is where the conflict lives and breathes, and by doing so, takes air out of the room the protagonist desperately needs. This is where the readers learn more about the individual relationships with the characters introduced in Act One. These complicate matters for the protagonist, but aren't necessarily bad. A love may deepen. A personal history may be revealed.

The Darkest Moment is where all the strings become so entangled we fear they are knotted beyond repair. How can the protagonist possibly get past this emotional or physical obstacle, this impediment? The protagonist is crushed. We are desperate to find a solution, only to realize one doesn't exist. Houdini is in the chains and under water, and the key he is supposed to have hidden down his throat has been swallowed.

Immediately after the Darkest Moment, the character has an epiphany, an inspiration, or draws upon something he remembers or has experienced in his past. A Discovery. This kicks off **Act Three**, when the conflicts begin to resolve. The resolution of these secondary conflicts is critical here, to make way for the operatic aria—the Climax. This needs to fly solo. In the climax, he deals, once and for all, with the central external conflict, and he takes a good look at his internal flaws. This is when he either succumbs to his failings or overcomes them. The reader is cheering for him to overcome his flaws, but characters do whatever they do. The point is that he must look at himself and be changed by what he sees. This will allow him to resolve the conflict (or not).

In the final analysis, readers will remember what happens to the protagonist internally, which is ultimately more important than what happens to the external conflict. The Discovery has led to resolution of the Conflict, has led to wisdom. Flawed wisdom, perhaps, but a wisdom we can understand that makes sense as a logical outcome of the Quest.

A story can be told from any point of view, can include any number of characters, can span any length of time, can host a number of subplots. Stick to one good guy, one bad guy, and one main point of conflict. Give your characters passion, memorable names, quirks, angers, frustrations and depth. Include lots of sensory imagery, so the reader can be in the scene with the character, and reveal your character's nature through the use of facial expressions and gestures. Differentiate the characters from each other, and from you. Give them a serious problem, throw them off the deep end, and watch them work their way out of it, given who they are and what they do.

Character

This is who we're dealing with. This is the person into whose shoes the reader will step for the duration of the story, so be sure he's interesting. Make certain this character is not you. Make this character a little bit larger than life. Exaggerate her personality attributes. Readers want conflict, excitement, entertainment. Reading about normal people won't cut it. Make sure your character has flaws and does things that fascinate your reader. Remember that your reader, tucked safely in bed, is living vicariously through that character. Give your reader a good ride by carefully drawing a very interesting character with likes and dislikes, habits, pet peeves, personality disorders. Make them sympathetic enough so that your reader roots for them to overcome their issues and find happiness (or love), but make those characters their own worst enemy. Instead of reading for pleasure, read to study classic characters, both protagonists and antagonists, and figure out why they have captured the attention of the reading public. Render them artfully, and with your reader as co-author (they will fill in any details you omit), put them into some serious conflict and let the fun begin.

- Choose your characters' names correctly.
- Know their families.
- One protagonist—a flawed, sympathetic, reluctant hero.
- One antagonist, obsessed.
- Beware of fun characters who pop up and want to take over the story, and deal with them accordingly.
- Don't be afraid to write from the point of view of someone of the opposite sex, but be careful. Be humble and do your research. Don't assume you know how the other half thinks.
- Reveal character at every opportunity: through their hands, a tool, the way they treat children, an animal, a member of their family, or the server in a restaurant.
- Build their character in dialogue with facial expressions and gestures.

- Respect that they are the heroes of their own story.
- Know their ghosts.
- Know and reveal their pet peeves, likes, dislikes, phobias, fears, dreams.
- Mix and match characteristics, using greater or lesser degrees of the Seven Deadly Sins: Anger, Greed, Pride, Lust, Envy, Gluttony and Sloth; and the Seven Principal Virtues: Prudence, Temperance, Fortitude, Justice, Faith, Hope, and Charity.
- Differentiate them from you and from each other. Radically.
- Give them different problem solving methods, vocabularies, politics.
- Characters must have something at stake. They can't just shrug and walk away.
- Characters must be correctly motivated to act the way they do.
- Reveal their sexual nature. Although you don't have to write sex scenes to reveal your characters' sexual nature, you might do it anyway, just because it's fun.
- Make them larger than life. Good guys are really good; bad guys are really bad. Be careful you don't make them into cartoons.
- Know their inner needs. That's what motivates them.

Point of View

Choosing the point of view (POV) from which your story will be told is the first important decision in designing your novel.

While this is in no way an exhaustive study of point of view, these are your basic options:

First Person - The whole story is told through the eyes of one character, using the pronoun "I." Most first-person novels are short, because this is such a restrictive platform. First person point of view is ideal for the detective mystery, because the reader learns all the clues simultaneously with the detective, and the race is on between the detective or the sleuth and the reader to solve the crime. (Note: The artful author will let the reader figure it out one page before the detective does. That lets the reader feel smart, he or she has had a good reading experience, and will likely pick up your next mystery.) The emotion, thoughts, actions, and personality of the viewpoint character are immediate and intimate. It's all told in his voice. The problem with first person is that the point of view character is the only one the reader gets to understand deeply.

I should have known when I took this job it wasn't going to be all cake and cocktails. In retrospect, I guess I did know. I just didn't pay attention to that little angel inside my head telling me this whole scene and everybody in it was going to turn into nightmare stuff.

Michelle sidled up and leaned on my arm. She was a great leaner. In her sultry voice she whispered,

"Mad at me?"

I wasn't exactly certain about her relationship to all these people, but I told myself she couldn't be part of it. Not the way she smelled. She couldn't be part of that rotten group. "No," I said, breathing her sweet, cinnamon fragrance. "I've just made another in a lifelong series of miscalculations."

Third Person Omniscient - "Omniscient" means all-knowing, all-seeing, like God. This viewpoint assumes access to every character's innermost thoughts, feelings and motivations. It also includes knowledge of the past and future.

This is a wide-open, loose way of writing. The disadvantage is that it often gives too much information. Using this point of view to introduce four characters in the first chapter, for example, may confuse your readers. But proper pacing and balanced writing will render this an entertaining and educational approach.

On the last day of Henry's life, he pulled into the library parking lot with a diamond in his pocket and a pounding in his heart. He was going to ask Lila Jane to be his wife, and he had been rehearsing his question all morning.

Lila Jane knew something was up with Henry. She worried about it as she waited just inside the glass library doors for him and his little Chevy. He'd been acting strange lately, and she was afraid he was going to tell her, as so many men had before, that he'd met someone else. Lila Jane felt that she was a fine woman and not a bad catch, but she seemed to have been born under an unlucky-in-love star.

Henry had just been born under an unlucky star.

Third Person Limited Omniscient - This is the most conventional point of view, and the most powerful. With this option, you write from one person's point of view at a time. If it's Stan's POV, you know his thoughts, feelings, emotions—the entire body of his knowledge. Stan feels angry, his blood pressure rises, fists clench, but you don't know how Matthew is feeling; you just know that, as Stan sees it, Matthew is being very quiet.

When you restrict your point of view to one person at a time, the writing becomes stronger. You may switch from Stan's to Matthew's POV whenever you need to pass along information that only Matthew can provide. Switching points of view can be disorienting to the reader, so do it dramatically (never in the middle of a paragraph) and ground the reader immediately in time and space and POV whenever there is a change.

Take time introducing the leading players on your novel's stage, and give them strong stimuli for action. That way your readers will remember each character for his personality and for the unique way he deals with the peculiar difficulties that befall him.

Matthew poured himself a generous portion of Scotch and flopped down in the leather recliner to drink it. Vague lights from the city below his high-rise apartment filtered through the vertical blinds, painting light stripes along the wall that held over thirty thousand dollars worth of stereo gear. Matthew was a success in business, and there was part of the proof. He had made a million dollars before he was thirty, made his second million before he was thirty-three. He had an investment portfolio that still amazed him, he had a seven-room Manhattan apartment, he drove a Rolls. He had a butler. He had everything, everything he thought he would need to impress his father and make the old man sit up and take notice.

But did he? No. Stanford didn't care about Matthew, and that ground glass in the pit of Matthew's stomach. What was it going to take?

Maybe nothing, he told himself. *Maybe Dad is incapable of acknowledging my success.*

But that wasn't it; he knew it wasn't. His father, the prestigious Stanford J. Prescott of Prescott Industries, was punishing Matt, and he'd keep it up to his dying breath and beyond.

Matt slugged down the liquor, felt it warm his

stomach, and rocked gently in the dim light of the room. There was nothing he could do about it, he told himself, just as he had told himself a million times before in the past twenty years.

The phone rang, and Matt looked over at it. There wasn't anybody he was interested in talking with, so he'd let it ring. He was enjoying his own company and his fine taste in Scotch.

Detached Narrative Voice - This is an impersonal, objective assessment of the scene. You can say what people do, but not what they think or how they feel. This, too, is a very restrictive point of view that doesn't gain your characters any sympathy with your readers. The best use of this point of view is to be interspersed with the others for a change in the texture of your book.

The boardroom was silent and sterile, with glass walls, dimmed lights and the eleven perfectly-situated leather chairs that surrounded the highly polished table. At the head of the table was the throne, a chair larger than any of the others, because that's how Stanford J. Prescott held his edge over the other board members. He was the king, he would always be the king, and they were not to forget it, not for a moment.

In front of each chair was a small, green-glass shaded lamp, a leather portfolio and a pen, all lined up with such precision that Prescott's secretary used a ruler to dress the room. Prescott always made certain the room made its all-important first impression. He checked it personally before every meeting. No stray hair, not a speck of dust, not a fingerprint. Nothing personal. This was business, and business was not personal. Business was cruel, and Stanford thrived on the precision it required.

Chances are, unless you're using the first person point of view, you will use multiple viewpoints in your book. This is fine. It is conventional. The design element comes in when you think about how to switch your points of view. Use rhythm. Minor, throwaway characters shouldn't be point of view characters. You can alternate points of view among all your point of view characters, or choose just one or two. But if you switch point of view, don't do it just once. Each point of view character should be heard from more than once.

You'll find a rhythm as you go along.

Suspense

Suspense is drawing out action.

It does no good to have the bad guy walk up to the victim, do his nefarious deed, and then walk out the door.

But if the innocent victim comes home, is alone, and we see the bad guy approaching slowly, ever so slowly, from the back bedroom while she's humming happily to herself in the kitchen, we have suspense. Draw out the scene. Let the reader worry. Turn all the sensory elements dark to reflect the action. Read some thrillers and study the way the authors use suspense.

Sexual tension can be very suspenseful. Draw it out. Make them long for one another. Make the readers worry that they'll never get together.

Setting/Environment

Readers need to be able to place themselves in the shoes of the characters. They must know what it feels like to be in the physical space that the character occupies. You might not need to describe the interior of a car, as that's a pretty familiar place, or a hospital room, or a grocery store, but other than that, be sure your reader knows exactly what is happening to the characters at all times. Readers are smart; they will accumulate sensory details to build a scene, so you don't have to devote page after page to atmosphere, but do put a sensory image in every paragraph. The reader (your co-author) will use those to build the scene. Be sure to use all five senses.

Final Draft

I don't know about you, but my first drafts are a mess. They are big, ugly, misshapen, hairy things, and that is, in part, because once I begin writing a first draft, I do not go back to fix anything. I make notes instead about things that need to be fixed in the next run-through. So my first drafts are full of clichés, erroneous information, and side trips that seemed like a good idea at the time I was writing them, but will eventually be taken out.

I write in complete drafts, separated by two weeks to let the work cool. When my *story* is right, and the book looks good, then I do a final draft.

This is my checklist:

- Take out all side trips. If it doesn't further the plot, it doesn't belong, no matter how well written.
- Flesh out the areas where you've been telling and not showing.
- Take out every use of these words: very, causing, here, this, now, today, just. Some of these are present tense words, and I'm always writing in the past tense.
- Investigate every use of the word "it." There is usually a better word.
- Investigate every sentence that begins "There is…" or "There are…" This indicates a weird point of view.
- Investigate every adverb. Try to pump up the verb instead.
- Replay carefully every conversation to make certain the person speaking is attributed correctly.
- Take out all qualifiers: almost, kind of, nearly, sort of. Pump up the action, the drama.
- Look for *anything* that might distract the reader, and fix it.
- Make sure the reader is grounded in space and time at every jump.

- Investigate every use of the verb "to be," (is, was, are, be, being, am, were) and gerunds. "He *was running* to the store." vs. "He *ran* to the store."
- Investigate every use of passive voice, looking for the telltale "by" construction. "The ball was hit by the boy." vs. "The boy hit the ball."
- Make sure every sentence furthers the story.
- Make sure every chapter has a structure and is weighted at the end.
- Make sure your opening grabs the reader and flows smoothly into the rest of the story.
- Make sure your ending echoes the beginning.
- Make sure your protagonist has an internal revelation separate from his external problem solving.
- Make sure ancillary characters don't take over the show.
- Take out clichés.
- Be interesting with every sentence.
- Vary the rhythm of your sentences—not all short, not all long.
- Put a sensory image in *every* paragraph. Don't forget that we currently have five.
- Make sure that the only thing that slows the plot is a subplot complication, and not description.
- Can you heighten the tension? Tighten the suspense? Do it.
- Have you answered all the questions your story posed to the reader? Double-check.

- Omit unnecessary words. (Thanks, Strunk and White!)
- In the final analysis, it should read like the wind.

Creative Compost File

Keep a file folder of things that amuse you. Write down interesting names on scraps of paper and put them in the Creative Compost File. Tear articles out of newspapers and magazines. If you do a ten-minute warm-up exercise with your internal editor turned off (highly recommended), sometimes you'll bite into something juicy. Put it in your Compost File. Plot ideas, character sketches, random bits of this or that, everything that may someday pertain to something you write—it all goes into the file.

I never refer to anything in the Compost File (except perhaps my list of interesting names), but I clean it out every decade or so, when it becomes so big that it threatens to take over valuable file drawer space. When I do, I am always amazed at the fact that I have used many of the things I put aside, and done it having forgotten completely that those tidbits were in there.

I think it's much like a dream. If you don't tell it to someone, you forget it by lunch time. The very act of re-reading it and putting it into the Compost File cements it in the subconscious, where it just sits and works, like all good compost, turning into creative gold.

"Only the united beat of sex and heart together can create ecstasy." —Anaïs Nin

Chapter 12 — Resources

Books to Inspire Erotic Writings

Erotica—the entire range of it—is easily accessible on the internet. Just go to Amazon.com and type in "erotica" under books and you'll find thousands of titles.

As with all things, most will not be to your taste. This list of classics is meant to be a jumping off point for you to start in your erotic readings/writings. It doesn't even begin to touch the explosion of gay, lesbian and bisexual literature. Explore online and local new and used bookstores for additional titles. Remember, some of these books might not be to your taste.

Erotica by Charlotte Hill and William Wallace

Joy of Sexual Fantasy by Dr. Andrew Stanway

Slow Hand edited by Michele Slung

My Secret Garden and *Forbidden Flowers* by Nancy Friday

Exit to Eden by Anne Rice writing as Anne Rampling

Vox by Nicholson Baker

Erotic Interludes edited by Lonnie Barbach

Pleasures: Women Write Erotica edited by Lonnie Barbach

Ladies Own Erotica and *Look Homeward Erotica* by Kensington Ladies Erotica Society

Deep Down, edited by Laura Chester

The Joy of Sex and *More Joy of Sex* by Alex Comfort

Cities of the Interior and *Delta of Venus* by Anaïs Nin

The Art of Sexual Ecstasy by Margo Anand

Erotica: Women's Writing from Sappho to Margaret Atwood by Margaret Reynolds

New Age Tantra Yoga by Howard John Zitko

The War Between the Sheets by Jerry Rubin and Mimi Leonard

Woman in the Window edited by Pamela Pratt

Sex and Sacred Games by Renate Stendahl

Touching Fire –Erotic Writings by Women edited by Thornton, Sturdevant and Sumrall

Best Women's Erotica annual series with various editors

Best American Erotica series edited by Susie Bright

How to be a Great Lover by Lou Paget

Quiver by Tobsha Learner

Intelligent Books on Writing

The Writers Journey by Christopher Vogler (I consider this mandatory reading for every writer)
Sometimes the Magic Happens by Terry Brooks
Write Away by Elizabeth George
Bird by Bird by Anne Lamott
On Writing by Stephen King
Writing Down the Bones by Natalie Goldberg

A Critique Group Format

Since I am a believer in writers belonging to a critique group, I'm including an example format. This is only one example of the way a critique group can work. It is designed to minimize the author ego factor, but no matter what format you choose, each member must be responsible to get their own value from the group. Don't go to a group because they need you. Go because you need them. Use the meeting time as a deadline to produce pages, listen to what your peers have to say about what you have written, take what you need and leave the rest.

This format was adapted from *The Teacherless Writing Class* by Peter Elbow:

1. A starting group should number three, four or five.
2. Go by the rules specifically for the first ten weeks.
3. Meet once a week for ten weeks. Each member of the group must solidly commit to attending each session. The group is effective only with group members who will make these sessions a priority.
4. Meet at the same place each week, preferably with privacy and without interruptions. Each person always sits in the same place.
5. The first person reads *with no introduction to the work except title*, for no more than ten minutes. All other participants listen. There is a brief pause, maybe five

seconds, then the writer reads the piece again. During the second run-through, other participants are allowed to take notes. Nothing is ever copied or passed around.

6. In a clockwise rotation, participants give their reaction to the piece as *readers*, not as writers. Comments should cover continuity, motivation, believability, structure, organization, but should steer clear of judging the subject matter. *Reactions are limited to two minutes.* There is no cross-table discussion. After everyone has finished with their 2-minute critique, there is a two-minute period for all participants (including the writer) to discuss the work. The entire process has taken a half hour, assuming a group of five.

7. Then the next person in the clockwise rotation takes their turn reading. The person who begins the session one week is last the following week.

8. Stick to this regimen exactly for ten weeks. At that time, discuss what would be best for your group (and you) and modify the rules accordingly.

9. If, after ten weeks, you decide to change the format, watch carefully for problems. If attendance goes down, productivity falls off, arguments ensue or personality problems arise, be willing to return to the original format. It works.

Afterword

Why do we write?

Human beings are incredibly complex. Most of the time we don't even understand ourselves, much less the other humans with whom we travel this journey on this planet.

Writing is a process by which we can answer the unanswerable questions about ourselves. We don the skin of a character (who is of us, but yet not us) and we throw them into situations that we find difficult, challenging, or abhorrent, and we watch our characters (ourselves) as they endeavor to climb their way out. We watch them make decisions that we would never make and watch them reap the rewards, or suffer the consequences. And by so doing, we not only hold the mirror to ourselves, but speak our truth.

Writing is a calling. We write because we must.

Why do we read?

We read because we lead lives of desperate calm. We go to great lengths to avoid conflict, yet fiction is all about conflict. When we go to bed at night and pick up a book, we slide into the clothing of a character embroiled in outrageous conflict and we learn about ourselves as we watch that character act — or fail to act — in ways we would — or we would not — and cheer as they triumph or despair as they fail. Along the way we say to ourselves, "I would never do that," or "I would love to do that," all the while knowing we would never, could never. This is the nature of escapist literature; we learn about ourselves as we live vicariously through the thrilling escapades of others.

Reading is a passion. We read because we must.

Therefore

We must work hard to satisfy the conditions set forth. We must delve into the psyches of our characters and explain them so fully to the reader that the reader learns something about his/herself and about the nature of humans. We need not take ourselves seriously, but we do need to take the work seriously. What we do as the keepers of the literature and the chroniclers of our times is important work. So do it well. Make it matter. Challenge yourself with every project and challenge your reader as well.

This is not easy, but it is worthwhile.

And sometimes, like when you're writing a sex scene, it's very, very fun.

About the Author

Elizabeth Engstrom is a sought-after teacher and keynote speaker at writing conferences, conventions, and seminars around the world. She has a BA in Literature/Creative Writing, and an MA in Applied Theology, both from Marylhurst University. Her hilarious workshops on writing a sex scene are a sought-after staple at writing conferences and conventions. She lives in the Pacific Northwest with her fisherman-husband and their dog where she is on the board of directors for Wordcrafters in Eugene (www.wordcraftersineugene.org). She teaches the occasional writing class, puts her pen to use for social justice, and is always working on her next book. www.ElizabethEngstrom.com

Books from IFD Publishing

Paperbacks

Novels:
Death is a Star by Christina Lay
Baggage Check by Elizabeth Engstrom

Nonfiction:
How to Write a Sizzling Sex Scene by Elizabeth Engstrom
The Surgeon's Mate: A Dismemoir by Alan M. Clark

EBooks

(You can find the following titles at most distribution points for all ereading platforms.)

Novels:
York's Moon, by Elizabeth Engstrom
Beyond the Serpent's Heart, by Eric Witchey
Lizzie Borden, by Elizabeth Engstrom
A Parliament of Crows by Alan M. Clark
Lizard Wine, by Elizabeth Engstrom
Northwoods Chronicles: A Novel in Short Stories, by Elizabeth Engstrom
Siren Promised, by Alan M. Clark and Jeremy Robert Johnson
To Kill a Common Loon, by Mitch Luckett
The Man in the Loon, by Mitch Luckett
Jack the Ripper Victim Series: Of Thimble and Threat by Alan M. Clark
Jack the Ripper Victim Series: The Double Event (includes two novels from the series: *Of Thimble and Threat* and *Say Anything But Your Prayers*) by Alan M. Clark
Candyland, by Elizabeth Engstrom
The Blood of Father Time: Book 1, The New Cut, by Alan M. Clark, Stephen C. Merritt & Lorelei Shannon
The Blood of Father Time: Book 2, The Mystic Clan's Grand Plot, by Alan M. Clark, Stephen C. Merritt & Lorelei Shannon

How I Met My Alien Bitch Lover: Book 1 from the Sunny World In-quisition Daily Letter
Archives, by Eric Witchey
Baggage Check, by Elizabeth Engstrom
Death is a Star, by Christina Lay
D. D. Murphry, Secret Policeman, by Alan M. Clark and Elizabeth Massie
Black Leather, by Elizabeth Engstrom

Novelettes:
The Tao of Flynn, by Eric Witchey
To Build a Boat, Listen to Trees, by Eric Witchey

Children's Illustrated:
The Christmas Thingy, by F. Paul Wilson. Illustrated by Alan M. Clark

Collections:
Suspicions, by Elizabeth Engstrom
Short Fiction:
"Brittle Bones and Old Rope," by Alan M. Clark
"Crosley," by Elizabeth Engstrom
"The Apple Sniper," by Eric Witchey

Nonfiction:
How to Write a Sizzling Sex Scene by Elizabeth Engstrom

Audio Books from Amazon and Audible.com

Novels:
The Door That Faced West by Alan M. Clark, read by Charles Hinckley
Jack the Ripper Victim Series: Of Thimble and Threat by Alan M. Clark, read by Alicia Rose
Jack the Ripper Victim Series: Say Anything But Your Prayers by Alan M. Clark, read by Alicia Rose
Jack the Ripper Victim Series: The Double Event by Alan M. Clark, read by Alicia Rose

www.ingramcontent.com/pod-product-compliance
Lightning Source LLC
Chambersburg PA
CBHW071640050426
42443CB00026B/773